RADIOLOGY

COLORING BOOK

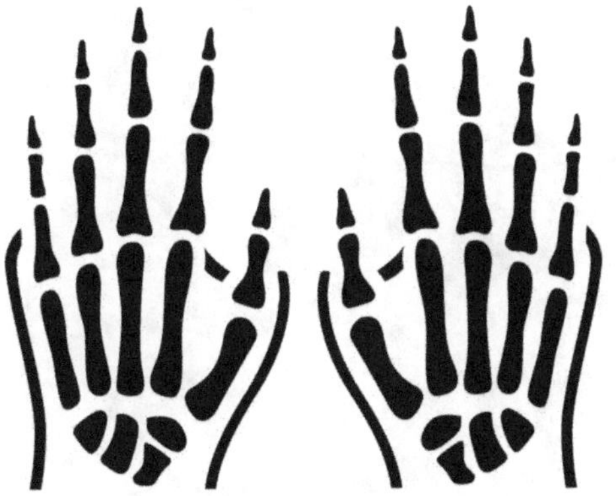

THIS BOOK BELONGS TO:

____

YOU SHOULD BE
Nice
TO ME
I CAN SEE RIGHT
THROUGH
You

I Can't Fix
Stupid
But I Can
X-RAY it

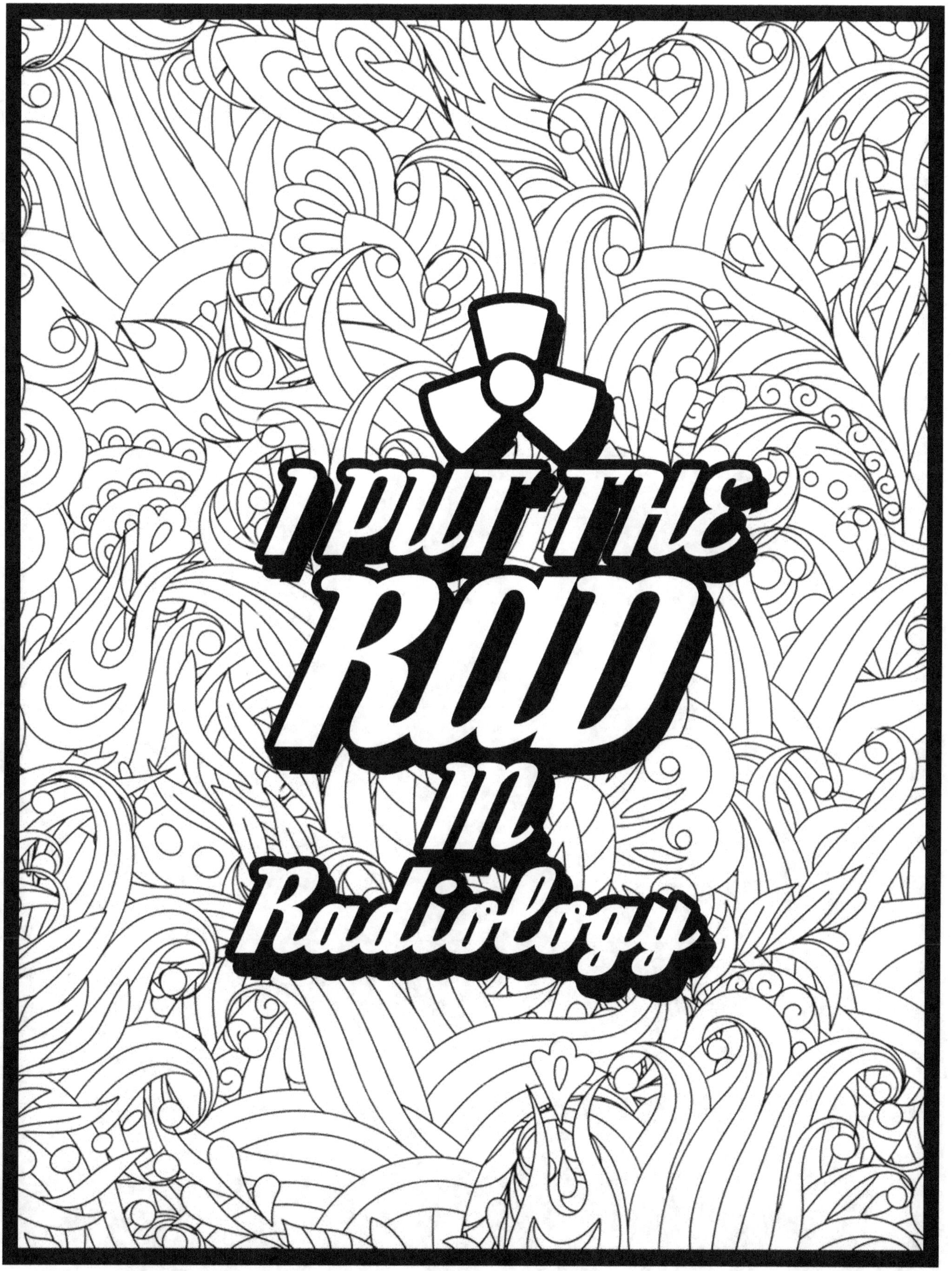
I PUT THE
RAD
IN
Radiology

HERE'S AN
X-RAY
OF THE
AMOUNT OF
F*CKS
I GIVE

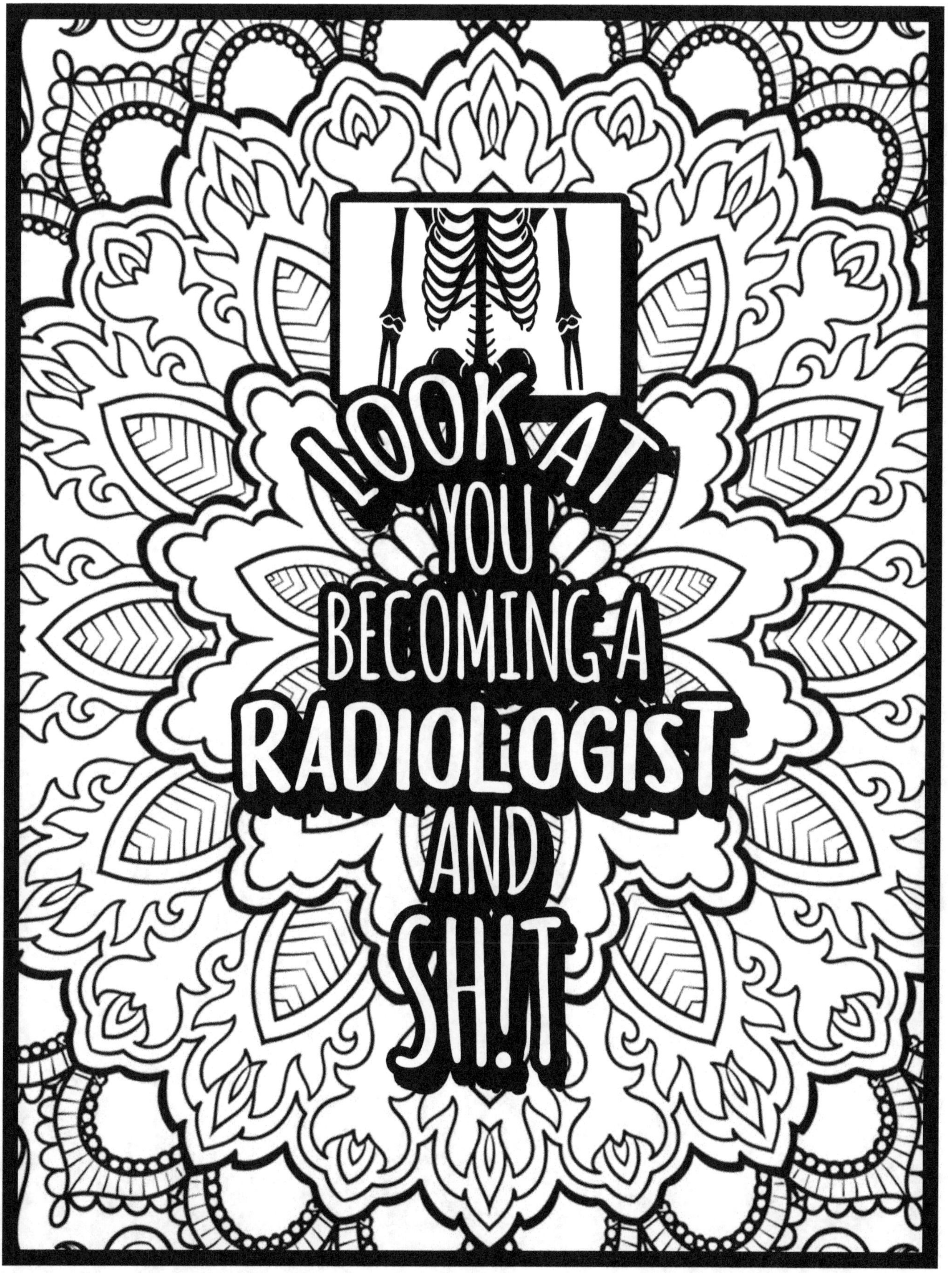
LOOK AT
YOU
BECOMING A
RADIOLOGIST
AND
SH!T

NOT ALL
PATIENTS
ARE IRRITATING
SOME ARE
UNCONSCIOUS

I'M A
RADIOLOGIST
WHAT'S YOUR
SUPER
POWER?

206
SHADES
OF
GREY!

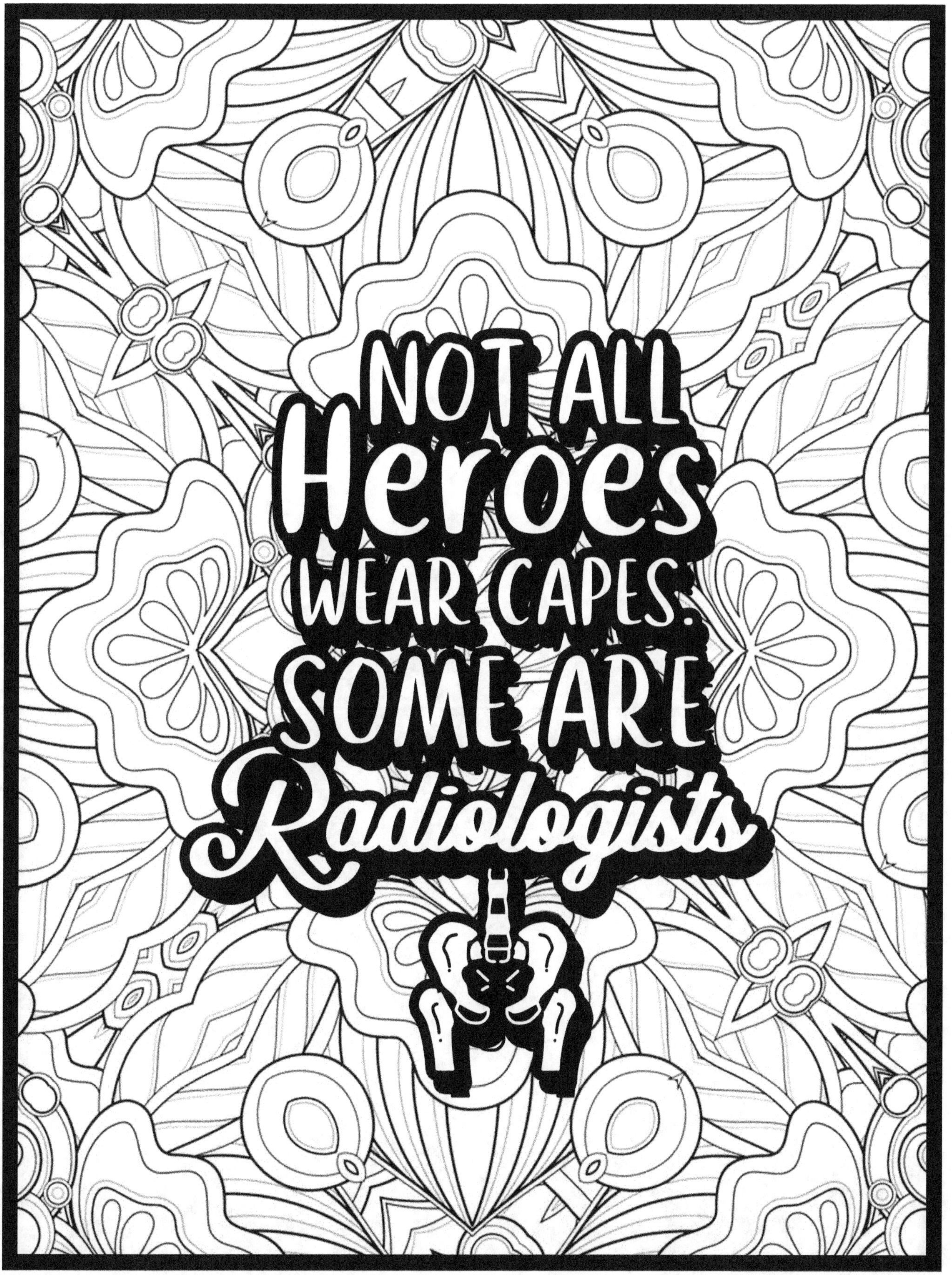
NOT ALL
Heroes
WEAR CAPES.
SOME ARE
Radiologists

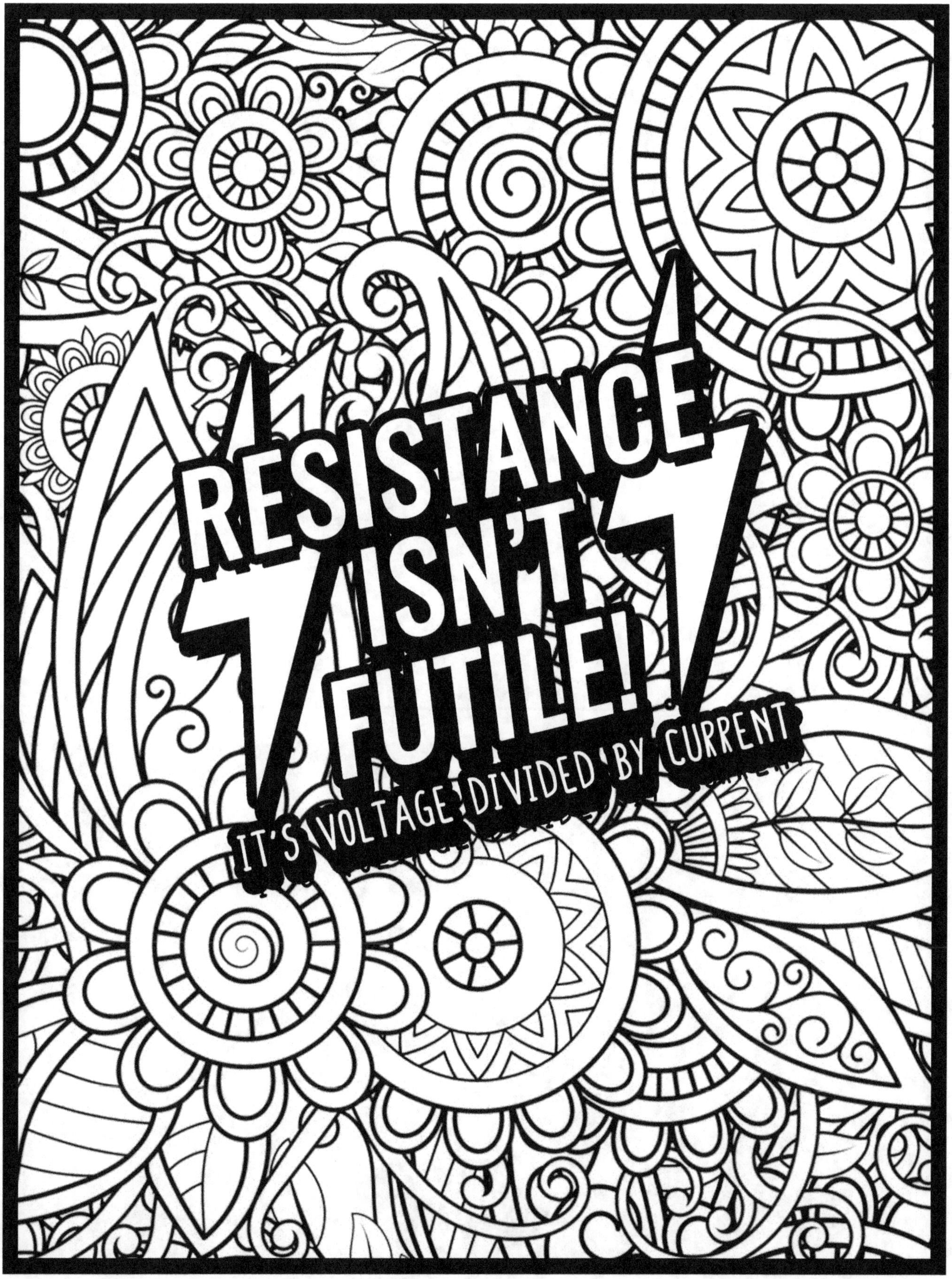
RESISTANCE ISN'T FUTILE!
IT'S VOLTAGE DIVIDED BY CURRENT

I'D AGREE
WITH YOU
BUT
THEN WE'D BOTH BE
WRONG!

I lost my
X-RAY
marker
THE REST OF MY DAY
is now
CRAP!

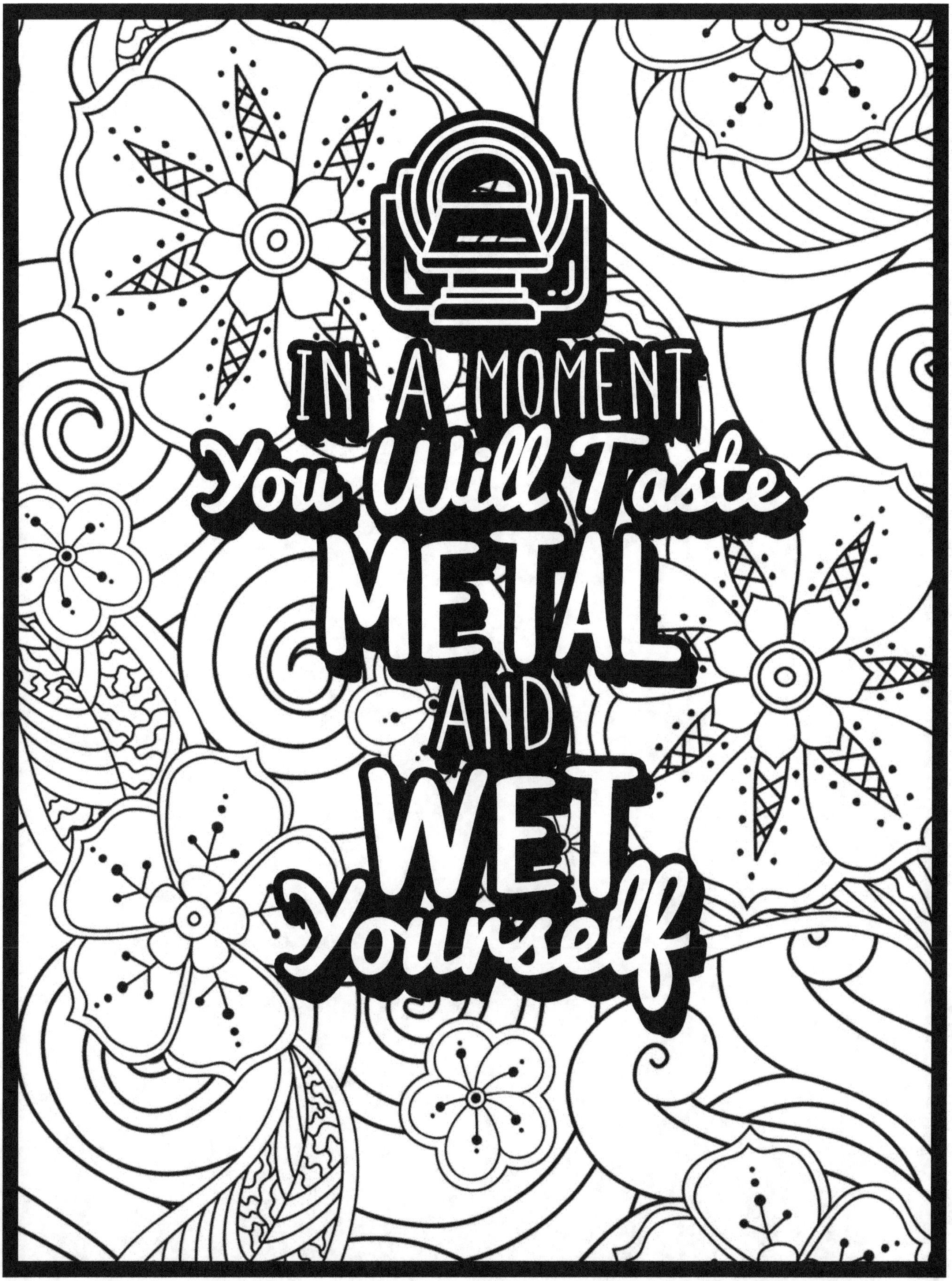
IN A MOMENT
You Will Taste
METAL
AND
WET
Yourself

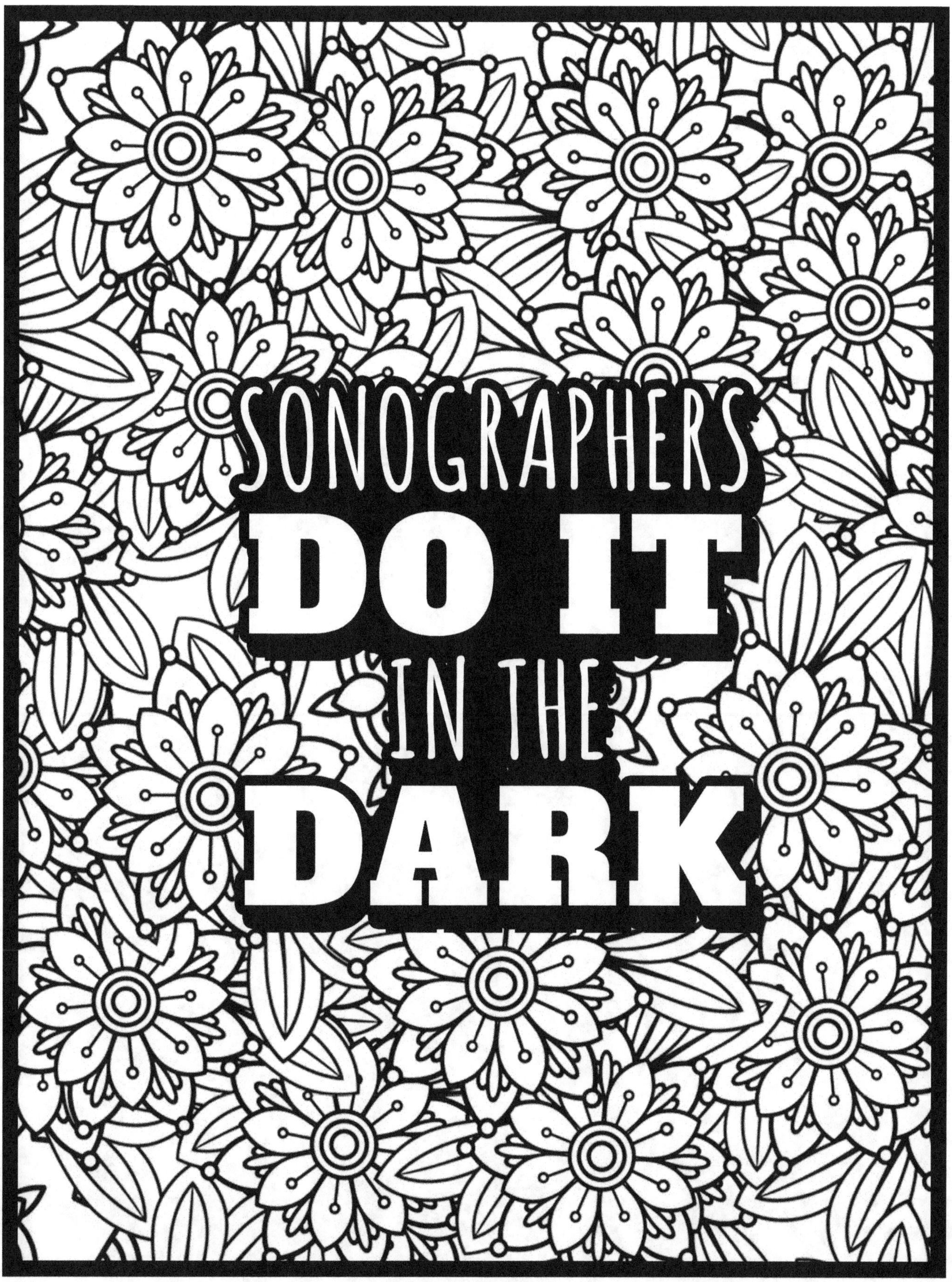
SONOGRAPHERS
DO IT
IN THE
DARK

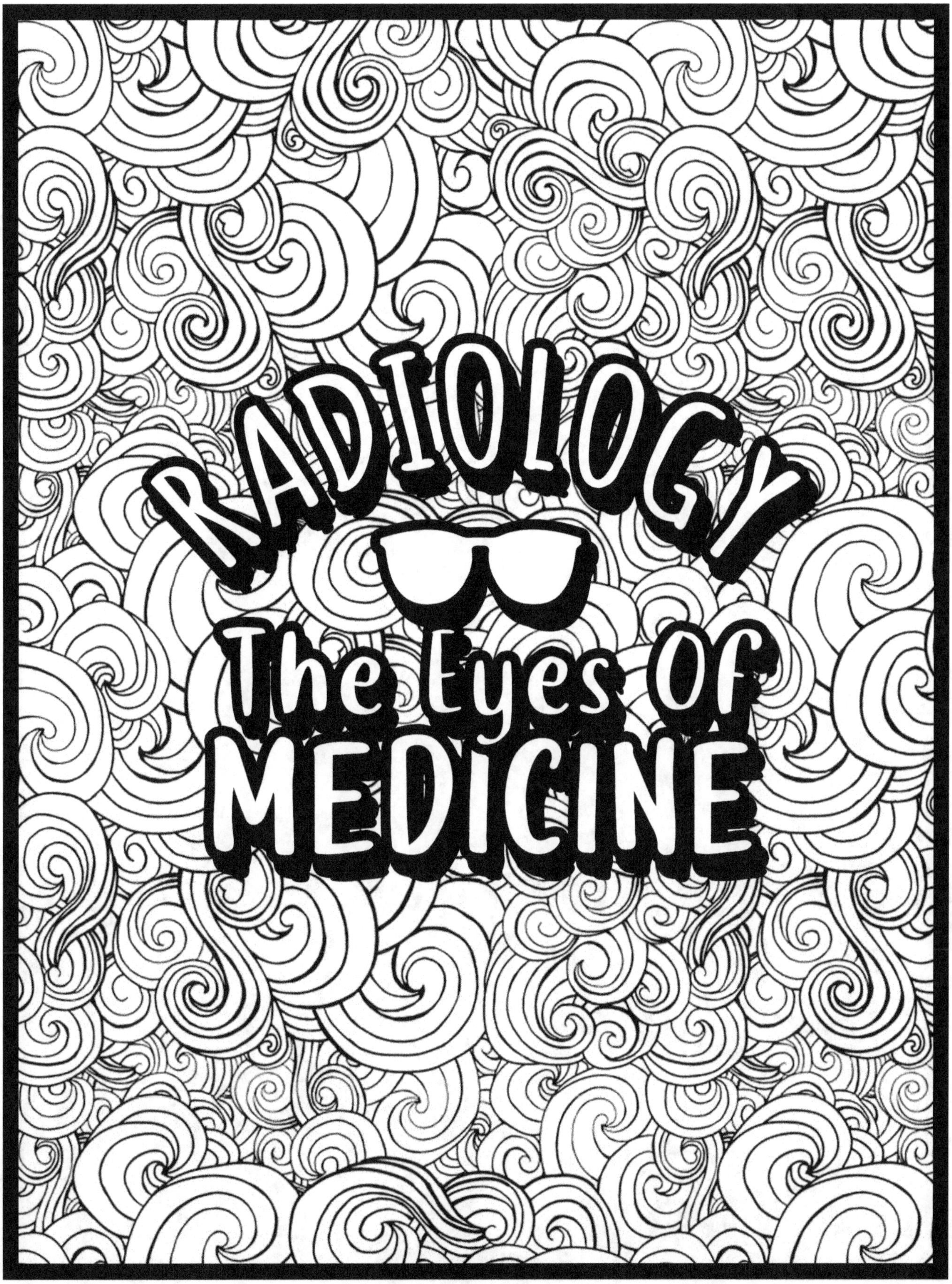
RADIOLOGY
The Eyes Of
MEDICINE

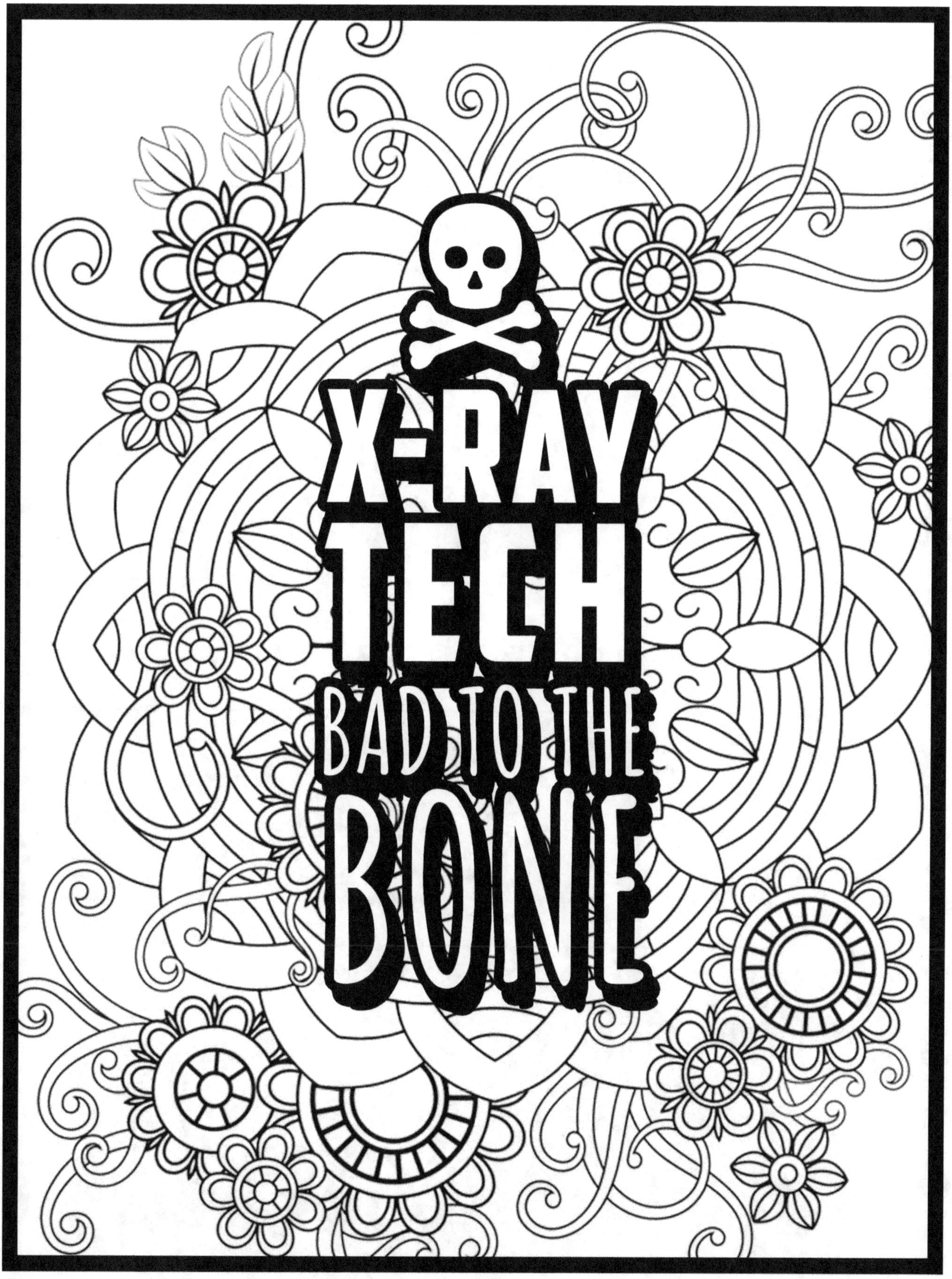
X-RAY
TECH
BAD TO THE
BONE

Merry
X-Raymas

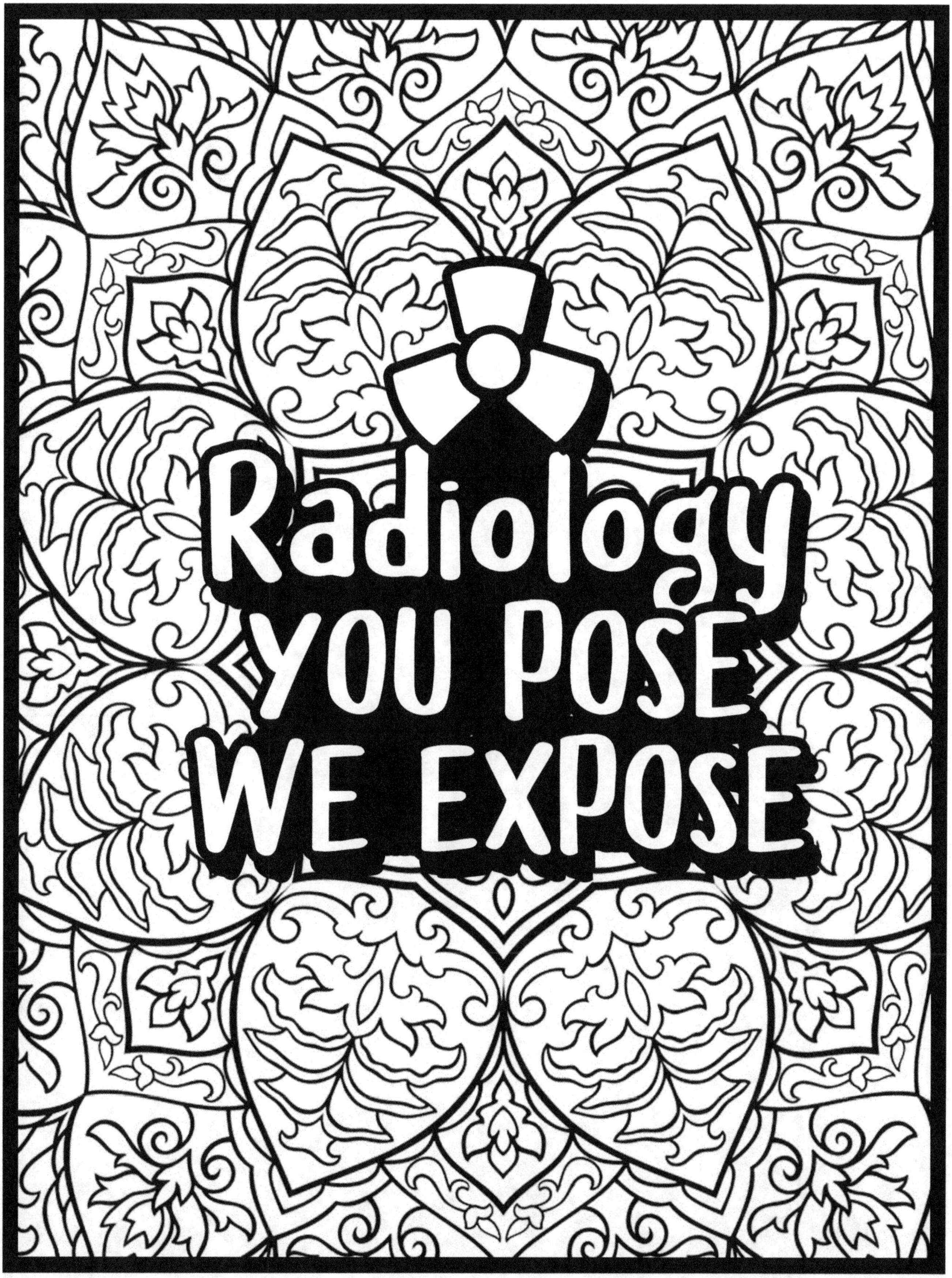
Radiology
YOU POSE
WE EXPOSE

Don't
Annoy me!
I Get Paid to
SHOOT PEOPLE
with
RADIATION

I'm not
Gonna Lie
THAT C'DIFF
SMELL IS REALLY ME!

www.ingramcontent.com/pod-product-compliance
Lightning Source LLC
Chambersburg PA
CBHW080628220526
45467CB00011B/3414
9798697771488